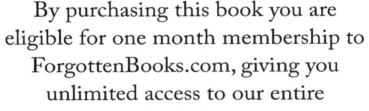

ISBN 978-1-397-31296-9
PIBN 11375044

COMMITTEES ON MILITARY MEDICINE

of the

DIVISION OF MEDICAL SCIENCES

NATIONAL RESEARCH COUNCIL

gust 1944

AVIATION MEDICINE
- ADVISORY COMMISSION A
- Acceleration
- Clothing
- Decompression Sickness
- Motion Sickness
- Oxygen and Anoxia
- Visual Problems

CHEMOTHERAPEUTIC AND OTHER AGENTS

CONVALESCENCE AND REHABILITATION

DRUGS AND MEDICAL SUPPLIES
- Essential Drugs
- Hospital and Surgical Supplies
- Medical Food Requirements
- Pharmacy

INDUSTRIAL MEDICINE
- Armored Vehicles

INFORMATION
- Historical Records
- Publicity

MEDICINE
- Cardiovascular Diseases
- Clinical Investigation
- Infectious Diseases
- Medical Nutrition
- Tropical Diseases
- Tuberculosis
- Venereal Diseases

NEUROPSYCHIATRY
- Neurology
- Psychiatry

PATHOLOGY

SANITARY ENGINEERING

SHOCK AND TRANSFUSIONS
- Blood Substitutes
- Shock

COMMITTEES ON MILITARY MEDICINE

AVIATION MEDICINE
- ADVISORY COMMISSION A
  - Acceleration
  - Clothing
  - Decompression Sickness
  - Motion Sickness
  - Oxygen and Anoxia
  - Visual Problems

CHEMOTHERAPEUTIC AND OTHER AGENTS

CONVALESCENCE AND REHABILITATION

DRUGS AND MEDICAL SUPPLIES
- Essential Drugs
- Hospital and Surgical Supplies
- Medical Food Requirements
- Pharmacy

INDUSTRIAL MEDICINE
- Armored Vehicles

INFORMATION
- Historical Records
- Publicity

MEDICINE
- Cardiovascular Diseases
- Clinical Investigation
- Infectious Diseases
- Medical Nutrition
- Tropical Diseases
- Tuberculosis
- Venereal Diseases

NEUROPSYCHIATRY
- Neurology
- Psychiatry

PATHOLOGY

SANITARY ENGINEERING

SHOCK AND TRANSFUSIONS
- Blood Substitutes
- Shock

COMMITTEES ON MILITARY MEDICINE

SURGERY
- Anesthesia
- Infected Wounds and Burns
- Neurosurgery
- Ophthalmology
- Orthopedic Surgery
- Otolaryngology
- Physical Therapy
- Plastic and Maxillofacial Surgery
- Radiology
- Thoracic Surgery
- Urology
- Vascular Injuries

TREATMENT OF GAS CASUALTIES

BOARD FOR THE COORDINATION OF MALARIAL STUDIES
- Clinical Testing of Antimalarials
- Pharmacology of Antimalarials
- Biochemistry of Antimalarials
- Synthesis of Antimalarials

COMMITTEES ON MILITARY MEDICINE

SURGERY

Anesthesia
Infected Wounds and Burns
Neurosurgery
Ophthalmology
Orthopedic Surgery
Otolaryngology
Physical Therapy
Plastic and Maxillofacial Surgery
Radiology
Thoracic Surgery
Urology
Vascular Injuries

TREATMENT OF GAS CASUALTIES

BOARD FOR THE COORDINATION OF MALARIAL STUDIES

Clinical Testing of Antimalarials
Pharmacology of Antimalarials
Biochemistry of Antimalarials
Synthesis of Antimalarials

INDEX OF COMMITTEE MEMBERS

NAME	PAGE
Abell	14
Abbott	16
Alexander	18
Allen	18
Alpers	12
Alving	20
Amberson	10
Avery	9
Babbitt	13
Baldes	1
Balfour	14
Ball	20
Bard	2,13,14
Barnes	8
Barr	19
Bastedo	5
Bazett	2
Beard	1
Benedict	16
Bennett	14,16
Bigger	18
Bishopp	13
Blake	3,9,20
Blalock	13,14
Blanchard	20,21
Bloomfield	8
Booth	14
Boothby	3
Boyd	10
Bowman	11
Braasch	18
Bronk	1,3,3
Brown, H.W.	10
Brown, J.M.	17
Buck	7
Butler, A.M.	20
Butler, T.C.	20
Caldwell	15
Cannon, P.R.	12
Cannon, W.B.	13
Carden	19
Chamberlain	18
Christie	18
Clark	19,19,20
Clarke	11
Coatney	19,20
Code	2
Coggeshall	19
Cohn	13
Cole	14
Coleman	15
Coller	4,5,14
Comroe	6
Conn	16
Cooper	20
Cope, O.	15
Cordes	16
Corner	7
Cort	10
Coulter	17
Cox	11
Cope, A.	21
Darrach	16
Davis, J.S.	17
Davis, Watson	7
DeGowin	13
Denny-Brown	1,1,2
de Takats	18
Dickson	16
Dietz	7
Dieuaide	19
Dochez	19
Douglas	10
Drake	21
Drinker, Cecil	1
Drinker, Philip	6,6
DuBois	1
Dubos	15
du Vigneaud	20
Eby	17
Edwards	10
Ehlers	13
Elderfield	21
Elman	4,15
Eloesser	18
Elvehjem	9
Ewerhardt	17
Fair	13
Ferris	2
Finnerud	5
Firor	15
Fishbein	4,7,7
Forbes	2
Fremont-Smith	12
Friedenwald	3
Fulton	1,2,7,7
Furstenberg	17
Gardner	10
Gayle	12
Geiling	20
Goodpasture	9
Gradle	16
Graham	4,14,18
Gregersen	14
Griffith	6
Guild	17
Hakansson	19
Hall	12
Hamer	18
Hansson	17
Harris, M.	2
Harris, T	12
Hartline	3
Harvey, E.N.	2
Hecht	3
Henry	7
Herring	7
Herrington	2
Herrmann	5
Hinman	18
Holmblad	6
Homans	18
Horrax	15
Howes	15
Huggins	18
Irons	4,5
Ivy, A.C.	2,9
Ivy, R.H.	14,17
Johnson, G.S.	1
Johnson, R.W.	4
Jolliffe	9
Jones, A.C.	17
Jones, T.D.	8
Karsner	12
Keefer	3,4,9
Kehoe	6
Kelly	4,6
Kennedy	11,12

NAME	PAGE
Kerr	1,2
Key	16
Kidner	16
King	9
Kirklin	18
Koch	15
Koepfli	21
Kretschmer	18
Krumbhaar	7
Krusen	17
Kubie	12
Landis	1,1
Laurence, W.L.	7
Lawrence, J	2
Leary	7,7
Lee, R.I.	8
Leadbetter	16
Le Jeune	17
Levy, G.J.	5
Levy, Robert	8
Lewis, J.K.	1,1
Lewis, L.L.	6
Lewis, N.D.C.	12
Lierle	17
Loeb	19,20,21
Lockwood	3,15
Long	9,14
Longcope	8
Lowery	17
Lund	15
Lundy	14
Lyman	2
MacKay	1,3
Mackenzie	4
Magnuson	16
Mahoney	11
Marshall	3,19,20
Marvel	19,21
Maurer	3
Maxcy	9,13
McCain	10
McClure	15
McCoy	19
McLester	9
Means	9
Meleney, F.	15
Meleney, H.	10
Merck	4
Meyer, A.	11
Meyer, K.F.	10
Miles	1,3
Mixter	14
Moore, J.E.	11
Moore, R.A.	12
Munger	5,5
Musser	4
Myers	10
Naffziger	14,15
Nelson	11
Newburgh	1,2,9
Newell	3
Newton	6
Norris	19
Nye	7
Ober	5,16
O'Brien	3
Ochsner	5,14
Osborne	6
Overholser	4
Palmer	4,5,8
Pappenheimer	12
Paullin	8
Pendergrass	18
Pepper	4,8
Pilcher	15
Pollock	12
Portmann	18
Porter, R.J.	20
Porter, W.B.	4
Post	16
Potter	7
Powers	6
Putnam	11,15
Raulston	1
Reese	16
Riley	12
Rioch	12
Robinson	2
Rovenstine	14
Ruedemann	16
Ruggles	11,12
Salter	7
Sawyer, W.A.	6
Schmidt, C.F.	3
Schmidt, C.L.A.	1
Schmidt, L.H.	20
Scholl	18
Schwab	12
Scott	8
Searle	4
Sebrell	19
Selby	6
Sevringhaus	9
Shannon	19,20
Shriner	21
Small	21
Smith, D.T.	9
Smith, Ferris	17
Smith, F.M.	8
Smith, G.M.	6,6
Smith-Petersen	16
Solomon	12
Sovatkin	5
Stare	9
Starr	4,5,6
Stead	5
Steckel	11
Stokes	11
Strecker	12
Striker	5
Strode	10
Stroud	4,5,8
Strumia	13
Sydenstricker	9
Taliaferro	10,20,20
Thomas	11
Thorn	9
Tillett	4
van Dyke	10
Van Slyke	13,20
Veal	18
Viets	7
Visscher	9
Wallerich	5
Wangensteen	13
Waring	10
Waters	14
Watson, C.J.	8
Watson, R.B.	10,20
Wearn	4,13,14

NAME	PAGE
Weech	10
Wendt	2
Whipple	14,15
White	8
Whitehorn	11
Whittaker	13
Wilder	8,9
Wilkins	1
Wilson	16
Winternitz	19
Wiselogle	21
Wolbach	12
Wolff	4
Wolman	13
Wood, P.M.	14
Woods	16
Woodward	17
Yaglou	2
Yant	6,6
Yater	8
Zeiter	17

INDEX TO COMMITTEES AND SUBCOMMITTEES

NAME	PAGE
Acceleration	1
ADVISORY COMMISSION A	1
Anesthesia	14
Armored Vehicles	6
AVIATION MEDICINE	1
Blood Substitutes	13
Biochemistry of Antimalarials	20
BOARD FOR THE COORDINATION OF MALARIAL STUDIES	19
Cardiovascular Diseases	8
CHEMOTHERAPEUTIC AND OTHER AGENTS	3
Clinical Investigation	9
Clinical Testing of Antimalarials	20
Clothing	2
CONVALESCENCE AND REHABILITATION	4
Decompression Sickness	2
DRUGS AND MEDICAL SUPPLIES	4
Essential Drugs	5
Historical Records	7
Hospital and Surgical Supplies	5
INDUSTRIAL MEDICINE	6
Infected Wounds and Burns	15
INFORMATION	7
Infectious Diseases	9
Medical Food Requirements	5
Medical Nutrition	9
MEDICINE	8
Motion Sickness	2
Neurology	12
NEUROPSYCHIATRY	11
Neurosurgery	15
Ophthalmology	16
Orthopedic Surgery	16
Otolaryngology	17
Oxygen and Anoxia	3
PATHOLOGY	12
Pharmacology of Antimalarials	20
Pharmacy	6
Physical Therapy	17

NAME	PAGE
Plastic and Maxillofacial Surgery	17
Psychiatry	12
Publicity	7
Radiology	18
SANITARY ENGINEERING	13
Shock	14
SHOCK AND TRANSFUSIONS	13
SURGERY	14
Synthesis of Antimalarials	21
Thoracic Surgery	18
TREATMENT OF GAS CASUALTIES	19
Tropical Diseases	10
Tuberculosis	10
Urology	18
Vascular Injuries	18
Venereal Diseases	11
Visual Problems	3

Note: All main committees appear in Capital Letters

NATIONAL RESEARCH COUNCIL - DIVISION OF MEDICAL SCIENCES
COMMITTEES ON MILITARY MEDICINE
1 August 1944
Dr. Lewis H. Weed, Chairman

AVIATION MEDICINE

Dr. Eugene F. DUBOIS	(Chm.), Prof. Physiology, Cornell Univ. Med. Coll. 1300 York Avenue, New York 21, N.Y.
Dr. Walter R. MILES	(Vice.Chm.), Prof. Psychology, Yale Univ. Sch. Med. 333 Cedar St., New Haven 11, Conn.
Dr. Detlev W. BRONK	Prof. Biophysics, Johnson Research Foundation, University of Pennsylvania, Philadelphia, Pa.
Dr. Derek DENNY-BROWN	Director, Neurological Unit Boston City Hospital, Boston, Mass.
Dr. Cecil K. DRINKER	Prof. Physiology, Harvard Medical School 55 Shattuck St., Boston 15, Mass.
Dr. John F. FULTON	Sterling Prof. Phys., Yale Univ. Sch. of Med. 333 ~~Cedar St., New Haven 11~~, Conn.
Dr. Eugene M. LANDIS	(Secy.), Prof. Physiology, Harvard Medical School 25 Shattuck St., Boston 15, Mass.
Dr. L. H. NEWBURGH	Prof. Clinical Investigation Univ. Mich. Sch. of Med., Ann Arbor, Mich.

ADVISORY COMMISSION A

Dr. J. K. LEWIS	(Chm.), Assoc. Prof. Med., Stanford Univ. Sch. Med. Stanford Univ. Hospitals, San Francisco, Calif.
Dr. Rodney BEARD	Asst. Prof. Pub. Health & Prev. Med. Stanford Univ. Pan American Airways, Treasure Island, San Francisco, Calif.
Dr. George S. JOHNSON	Prof. Med. (Neuropsych.) Stanford Univ. Sch. Med., San Francisco,15,Calif.
Dr. William KERR	Prof. Med., Univ. Calif. Med. Sch. Univ. Calif. Hospital, San Francisco,22, Calif.
Dr. Eaton MACKAY	Scripps ~~Metabolic Clinic~~, La Jolla, Calif.
Dr. B. O. RAULSTON	Prof. Med., Univ. South. Calif. Med. Sch. 1200 N. State St., Los Angeles, Calif.
Dr. Carl L. A. SCHMIDT	Prof. Biochemistry Univ. California, Berkeley, Calif.

Subcommittee on Acceleration

Dr. Eugene M. LANDIS	(Chm.), Prof. Physiology, Harvard Med. Sch. 25 Shattuck St., Boston 15, Mass.
Dr. E. J. BALDES	Vice Chairman, Exec. Board, Mayo Aeromedical Unit Mayo Foundation, Rochester, Minn.
Dr. Derek DENNY-BROWN	Director, Neurological Unit Boston City Hospital, Boston, Mass.
Dr. J. K. LEWIS	Assoc. Prof. Med., Stanford Univ. Sch. of Med. Stanford Univ. Hospitals, San Francisco, Calif.
Dr. Robert W. WILKINS	Asst. Prof. Med., Boston Univ. Sch. of Med. Mass. Memorial Hospitals, Boston, Mass.

Subcommittee on Clothing

Dr. L. H. NEWBURGH	(Chm.), Prof. Clinical Investigation Univ. Mich. Sch. Med., Ann Arbor, Mich.
Dr. H. C. BAZETT	Prof. Physiology Univ. Penna. Sch. Med., Philadelphia 4, Pa.
Dr. W. H. FORBES	Fatigue Laboratory Harvard University, Soldiers Field, Boston, Mass.
Dr. Milton HARRIS	Bureau of Standards Conn. at Upton St., N.W., Washington 25, D.C.
Dr. L. P. HERRINGTON	(Secy.), Assoc. Director John B. Pierce Foundation 290 Congress Ave., New Haven, Conn.
Dr. Sid ROBINSON	Assoc. Prof. Phys. Indiana Univ. Med. Sch., Bloomington, Ind.
Prof. C. P. YAGLOU	Assoc. Prof. Ind. Hyg., Harvard Med. Sch. 55 Shattuck St., Boston 15, Mass.

Subcommittee on Decompression Sickness

Dr. John F. FULTON	(Chm.), Sterling Prof. Phys., Yale Univ. Sch. Med. 333 Cedar St., New Haven 11, Conn.
Dr. C. F. CODE	Mayo Foundation, Rochester, Minn.
Dr. Eugene B. FERRIS	Prof. Med., Univ. Cincinnati Coll. Med. Cincinnati Gen. Hosp., Cincinnati 29, Ohio
Dr. E. Newton HARVEY	Prof. Physiology Princeton University, Princeton, N.J.
Dr. A. C. IVY	Northwestern Univ. Sch. of Med. 303 E. Chicago Ave., Chicago, Ill.
Dr. John LAWRENCE	Dir., Medical Research Crocker Radiation Lab., Berkeley, Calif.

Subcommittee on Motion Sickness

Dr. Derek DENNY-BROWN	(Chm.), Director, Neurological Unit Boston City Hospital, Boston, Mass.
Dr. Philip BARD	Prof. Physiology Johns Hop. Univ. Med. Sch. Baltimore 5, Md.
Dr. William KERR	Prof. Med., Univ. Calif. Med. Sch. Univ. Calif. Hospital, San Francisco 22, Calif.
Dr. Richard S. LYMAN	Prof. Neuro-Psych., Duke Univ. Med. Sch. Duke Hospital, Durham, N. C.
Dr. George Richard WENDT	Wesleyan University, Middletown, Conn.

Subcommittee on Oxygen and Anoxia

Dr. Detlev W. BRONK	(Chm.), Prof. Biophysics, Johnson Research Foundation, Univ. of Penna., Philadelphia, Pa.
Dr. Walter BOOTHBY	Prof. Med. & Biochem., Univ. Minn. Grad. Med. Sch. Mayo Clinic, Rochester, Minn.
Dr. Eaton MACKAY	Scripps Metabolic Clinic, La Jolla, Calif.
Dr. Frank W MAURER	Asst. Prof. Phys., Harvard Med. Sch. 55 Shattuck Street, Boston 15, Mass.
Dr. Carl F. SCHMIDT	Prof. Pharmacology Univ. Penna. Med. Sch., Philadelphia 4, Pa.

Subcommittee on Visual Problems

Dr. Detlev W. BRONK	(Chm.), Prof. Biophysics, Johnson Research Foundation, Univ. of Penna., Philadelphia, Pa.
Dr. Jonas FRIEDENWALD	Assoc. Prof. Ophth., Johns Hop. Univ. Sch. Med. Johns Hopkins Hospital, Baltimore 5, Md.
Dr. Haldan K. HARTLINE	Assoc. Prof. Biophysics Univ. Penna. Med. Sch., Philadelphia 4, Pa.
Dr. Selig HECHT	Prof. Biophysics Laboratory of Biophysics, Columbia University Broadway at 119th St., New York 27, N.Y.
Dr. Walter R. MILES	Prof. Psychology Yale Univ. Sch. of Med., New Haven 11, Conn.
Dr. Robert R. NEWELL	Prof. Med. (Radiology) Stanford Univ. Sch. Med., San Francisco, Calif.
Dr. Brian O'BRIEN	Prof. Physiological Optics Univ. Rochester, Rochester, N.Y.

CHEMOTHERAPEUTIC AND OTHER AGENTS

Dr. Chester S. KEEFER	(Chm.), Wade Prof. Med., Boston Univ. Sch. Med. 65 E. Newton St., Boston 18, Mass.
Dr. Francis G. BLAKE	Sterling Prof. Med. Yale Univ. Sch. of Med., New Haven 11, Conn.
Dr. John S. LOCKWOOD	(Secy.), Assoc. Prof. Surg., Yale Univ. Sch. Med. 2101 Constitution Ave., Washington 25, D. C.
Dr. E. K. MARSHALL, Jr.	Prof. Pharm. & Exp. Ther. Johns Hop. Univ. Sch. Med., Baltimore 5, Md.
Dr. W. Barry WOOD, Jr.	Department of Medicine, Washington Univ. Sch. Med. St. Louis, Mo.

CONVALESCENCE AND REHABILITATION

Dr. Wm. S. TILLETT	(Chm.), Prof. Med., N.Y. Univ. Coll. Med. 477 First Ave., New York 16, N.Y.
Dr. Robert ELMAN	Assoc. Prof. Clin. Surg., Wash. Univ. Sch. Med. 600 S. Kingshighway, St. Louis 10, Mo.
Dr. Robert W. JOHNSON, Jr.	4 E. Madison St., Baltimore, Md.
Dr. Geo. M. MACKENZIE	Assoc. Prof. Med., Albany Medical College Cooperstown, New York
Dr. Winfred OVERHOLSER	Prof. Psych., Geo. Wash. Univ. Sch. Med. St. Elizabeths Hospital, Washington 20, D.C.
Dr. Joseph T. WEARN	Prof. Med., Western Reserve Med. School 2065 Adelbert Road, Cleveland 6, Ohio
Dr. Harold G. WOLFF	Assoc. Prof. Med., Cornell Univ. Med. Coll. 525 E. 68th St., New York City

DRUGS AND MEDICAL SUPPLIES

Dr. W. W. PALMER	(Chm.), Bard Prof. Med., Col. Univ. Coll. Phys. & Surg. 622 W. 168th St., New York 32, N.Y.
Dr. Frederick A. COLLER	Prof. Surg., Univ. Mich. Med. Sch. 1313 E. Ann St., Ann Arbor, Mich.
Dr. Morris FISHBEIN	Editor, J.A.M.A. 535 N. Dearborn St., Chicago 10, Ill.
Dr. Evarts A. GRAHAM (ex officio)	Bixby Prof. Surg., Wash. Univ. Sch. of Med. 600 S. Kingshighway, St. Louis 10, Mo.
Dr. Ernest E. IRONS	Olin. Prof. Med., Rush Medical College 122 S. Michigan Ave., Chicago, Ill.
Dr. Chester S. KEEFER (ex officio)	Wade Prof. Med., Boston Univ. Sch. Med. 65 E. Newton Street, Boston 18, Mass.
Dr. E. F. KELLY	American Pharmaceutical Assn. 2215 Constitution Ave., Washington 25, D. C.
Mr. George W. MERCK	Merck & Co., Rahway, N.J.
Dr. J. H. MUSSER	Prof. Med., Tulane Univ. Med. Sch. 1430 Tulane Ave., New Orleans 13, La.
Dr. O. H. Perry PEPPER (ex officio)	Prof. Med., Univ. Pa. Sch. of Med. University Hospital 36th & Spruce Sts., Philadelphia 4, Pa.
Dr. William B. PORTER	Prof. Medicine Medical College of Virginia Hospital Division, Richmond, Va.
Mr. John G. SEARLE	G. D. Searle Company P. O. Box 5110, Chicago, Ill.
Dr. Isaac STARR	Prof. Therapeutics Univ. Pa. Sch. of Med., Philadelphia 4, Pa.
Dr. William D. STROUD	Prof. Cardiology, Univ. Pa. Grad. Med. Sch. 1011 Clinton St., Philadelphia, Pa.

Subcommittee on Essential Drugs

Dr. Ernest E. IRONS	(Chm.), Clin. Prof. Med., Rush Med. College 122 S. Michigan Ave., Chicago, Ill.
Dr. Walter A. BASTEDO	33 East 68th St., New York City
Dr. George R. HERRMANN	Prof. Int. Med. Univ. Texas Sch. of Med., Galveston, Texas
Dr. Isaac STARR	(Secy.), Prof. Therapeutics Univ. Pa. Sch. of Med., Philadelphia 4, Pa.
Dr. Eugene M. STEAD	Prof. Med., Emory Univ. Sch. of Med. 50 Armstrong St., Atlanta 3, Ga.

Subcommittee on Hospital and Surgical Supplies

Dr. Frederick A. COLLER	(Chm.), Prof. Surg., Univ. Mich. Med. Sch. 1313 E. Ann St., Ann Arbor, Mich.
Dr. C. W. MUNGER	Director St. Luke's Hospital Morningside Heights, New York City
Dr. Frank OBER	John Ball and Buckminster Brown Clin. Prof. Orth. Surgery, Harvard Medical School 234 Marlborough St., Boston, Mass.
Mr. Edward J. SOVATKIN	J. Sklar Manufacturing Co. 38-04 Woodside Ave., Long Island City, N.Y.
Mr. G. W. WALLERICH	V. Mueller & Company 408 S. Honore St., Chicago, Ill.

Subcommittee on Medical Food Requirements

Dr. William D. STROUD	(Chm.), Prof. Cardiology, Univ. Pa. Grad. Med. Sch. 1011 Clinton St., Philadelphia, Pa.
Dr. Clark W. FINNERUD	Asst. Prof. Derm., Univ. of Ill. 55 E. Washington St., Chicago, Ill.
Dr. Gilbert J. LEVY	Assoc. Prof. Ped., Univ. Tenn. Coll. of Med. 188 S. Bellevue Blvd., Memphis, Tenn.
Dr. C. W. MUNGER	Director St. Luke's Hospital Morningside Heights, New York City
Dr. Alton OCHSNER	Wm. Henderson Prof. Surg., Tulane Univ. Sch. Med. 1430 Tulane Ave., New Orleans 13, La.
Dr. W. W. PALMER (ex officio)	Bard Prof. Med., Col. Univ. Coll. Phys. & Surg. 622 W. 168th St., New York 32, N.Y.
Dr. Cecil STRIKER	630 Vine St., Cincinnati, Ohio

Subcommittee on Pharmacy

Dr. Isaac STARR	(Chm.), Prof. Therapeutics Univ. Pa. Sch. of Med., Philadelphia 4, Pa.
Dr. J. H. COMROE, Jr.	Univ. Pa. Sch. of Med., Philadelphia 4, Pa.
Dr. Ivor GRIFFITH	President Phila. Coll. of Pharmacy & Science 43rd St., Kingsessing & Woodland Aves. Philadelphia, Pa.
Dr. E. F. KELLY	American Pharmaceutical Assn. 2215 Constitution Ave., Washington 25, D. C.
Dr. Howard C. NEWTON	Dean Mass. Coll. of Pharmacy, Boston, Mass.
Dr. Justin POWERS	American Pharmaceutical Assn. 2215 Constitution Ave., Washington 25, D. C.

INDUSTRIAL MEDICINE

Dr. Clarence D. SELBY	(Chm.), Medical Director General Motors Corp., Detroit 2, Mich.
Prof. Philip DRINKER	Prof. Indus. Hyg., Harvard Medical School 55 Shattuck St., Boston 15, Mass.
Dr. E. C. HOLMBLAD	(Secy.), 28 E. Jackson St., Chicago, Ill.
Dr. Robert A. KEHOE	Res. Prof. Physiology Univ. Cinn. Coll. of Med., Cincinnati, Ohio
Dr. Earl D. OSBORNE	Prof. Derm. & Syph., Univ. Buffalo Sch. Med. 471 Delaware Ave., Buffalo 2, N.Y.
Dr. Wm. Alfred SAWYER	343 State St., Rochester, N.Y.
Dr. George M. SMITH	Res. Assoc. in Anat., Yale Univ. Sch. Med. 333 Cedar St., New Haven 11, Conn.
Mr. William P. YANT	Dir., Res. & Development Mine Safety Appliance Co. Braddock, Thomas & Meade Sts. Pittsburgh, Pa.

Subcommittee on Armored Vehicles

Dr. George M. SMITH	(Chm.), Res. Assoc. in Anat., Yale Univ. Sch. Med. 333 Cedar St., New Haven 11, Conn.
Prof. Philip DRINKER	Prof. Indus. Hyg., Harvard Med. Sch. 55 Shattuck St., Boston 15, Mass.
Mr. L. L. LEWIS	Vice President Carrier Corporation, Syracuse, N.Y.
Mr. William P. YANT	Dir., Res. & Development Mine Safety Appliance Co. Braddock, Thomas & Meade Sts. Pittsburgh, Pa.

INFORMATION

Dr. Morris FISHBEIN	(Chm.), Editor, J.A.M.A. 535 N. Dearborn St., Chicago 10, Ill.
Dr. John F. FULTON	Sterling Prof. Phys., Yale Univ. Sch. Med. 333 Cedar St., New Haven 11, Conn.
Mr. James C. LEARY	The Chicago Daily News 400 West Madison St., Chicago 6, Ill.
Dr. Robert N. NYE	Managing Editor, New England Journal of Medicine 8 Fenway, Boston 15, Mass.

Subcommittee on Historical Records

Dr. John F. FULTON	(Chm.), Sterling Prof. Phys., Yale Univ. Sch. Med. 333 Cedar St., New Haven 11, Conn.
Dr. Solon J. BUCK	Archivist of the U.S. The National Archives, Washington 25, D. C.
Dr. George W. CORNER	Carnegie Institution of Washington Dept. of Embryology Wolfe & Madison Sts., Baltimore 5, Md.
Mr. Pendleton HERRING	Exec. Secy. Committee on Records of War Admin. Grad. Sch. of Public Administration Harvard University, Cambridge, Mass.
Dr. Edward Bell KRUMBHAAR	Prof. Pathology Univ. Pa. Sch. of Med., Philadelphia 4, Pa.
Dr. Henry R. VIETS	Lect. on Neurology, Harvard Medical School 262 Beacon St., Boston, Mass.

Subcommittee on Publicity

Dr. Morris FISHBEIN	(Chm.), Editor, J.A.M.A. 535 N. Dearborn St., Chicago 10, Ill.
Mr. Watson DAVIS	Editor, Science Service & Science News Letter 1719 N St., N.W., Washington 6, D. C.
Mr. David DIETZ	Science Editor, Scripps-Howard Newspapers, United Press Cleveland Press Building, Cleveland, Ohio
Mr. H. J. HENRY	Director of Merchandising Johnson & Johnson, New Brunswick, N.J.
Mr. William L. LAURENCE	New York Times, New York City
Mr. James C. LEARY	The Chicago Daily News 400 West Madison St., Chicago 6, Ill.
Mr. Robert D. POTTER	Science Editor The American Weekly, 235 E. 45th St., New York City
Mr. Lawrence C. SALTER	Assoc. Dir., Press Relations, J.A.M.A. 535 N. Dearborn St., Chicago 10, Illinois

MEDICINE

Dr. O. H. Perry PEPPER	(Chm.), Prof. Med., Univ. Pa. Med. Sch. University Hospital 36th & Spruce Sts., Philadelphia 4, Pa.
Dr. A. L. BLOOMFIELD	Prof. Med., Stanford Univ. Sch. of Med., San Francisco, California
Dr. Roger I. LEE	Trustee, A.M.A. 264 Beacon St., Boston, Mass.
Dr. W. T. LONGCOPE	Prof. Med., Johns Hopkins Univ.Sch. Med. Johns Hopkins Hosp., Baltimore 5, Md.
Dr. W. W. PALMER	Bard Prof. Med., Col. Univ. Coll. Phys. & Surg. 622 West 168th St., New York 32, N.Y.
Dr. James E. PAULLIN	(Secy.), Prof. Clin. Med., Emory Med. School 384 Peachtree St., N.E., Atlanta 3, Ga.
Dr. Fred M. SMITH	Prof. Theory & Pract., State Univ. Iowa Coll. Med. University Hospitals, Iowa City, Iowa
Dr. C. J. WATSON	Prof. Medicine Univ. Minn. Med. Sch., Minneapolis, 14, Minn.
Dr. Russell M. WILDER	Prof. Med. & Nutr., Univ. Minn. Grad. Sch. Mayo Clinic, Rochester, Minnesota

Subcommittee on Cardiovascular Diseases

Dr. Paul Dudley WHITE	(Chm.), Lect. on Med., Harvard Medical School Mass. General Hosp., Boston, 14, Mass.
Dr. Arlie R. BARNES	Prof. Med., Univ. Minn. Grad. Med. Sch. Mayo Clinic, Rochester, Minn.
Dr. T. Duckett JONES	Asst. Prof. Med., Harvard Med. School 25 Binney St., Boston, Mass.
Dr. Robert L. LEVY	Prof. Clin. Med., Col. Univ. Coll. Phys. & Surg. 730 Park Avenue, New York City
Dr. Roy W. SCOTT	Prof. Clin. Med., Western Res. Univ. Sch. Med. 3395 Scranton Road, Cleveland, Ohio
Dr. William D. STROUD	(Secy.), Prof. Card., Grad. Med. Sch. Univ. Pa. 1011 Clinton St., Philadelphia, Pa.
Dr. Wallace M. YATER	Prof. Med., Georgetown Univ. Sch. Med. Georgetown Univ. Hosp., Washington 7, D. C.

Subcommittee on Clinical Investigation

Dr. J. H. MEANS	(Chm.), Jackson Prof. Clin. Med., Harvard Med. Sch. Massachusetts General Hospital, Boston, 14, Mass.
Dr. A. C. IVY	Northwestern Univ. Sch. of Med. 303 E. Chicago Ave., Chicago, Ill.
Dr. C. N. H. LONG	Sterling Prof. Phys. Chem. Yale Univ. Sch. of Med., New Haven 11, Conn.
Dr. L. H. NEWBURGH	Prof. Clin. Inv. Univ. Mich. Med. Sch., Ann Arbor, Mich.
Dr. Elmer L. SEVRINGHAUS	Prof. Med., Univ. Wisc. Med. Sch. 1300 University Ave., Madison 6, Wisc.
Dr. George W. THORN	(Secy.), Hersey Prof. of Theory and Practice of Physic, Harvard Medical School Peter Bent Brigham Hosp., Boston, Mass.
Dr. Maurice B. VISSCHER	Prof. Gen. Physiology Univ. Minn. Med. Sch., Minneapolis 14, Minn.

Subcommittee on Infectious Diseases

Dr. Francis G. BLAKE	(Chm.), Sterling Prof. Medicine Yale Univ. Sch. of Med., New Haven 11, Conn.
Dr. O. T. AVERY	Hospital of the Rockefeller Inst. for Med. Res. New York City
Dr. Ernest W. GOODPASTURE	Prof. Pathology Vanderbilt Univ. Sch. Med., Nashville, Tenn.
Dr. Chester S. KEEFER	(Secy.), Wade Prof. Med., Boston Univ. Sch. of Med. 65 E. Newton Street, Boston 18, Mass.
Dr. Kenneth F. MAXCY	Prof. Epidemiology School of Hygiene & Public Health Johns Hopkins University, Baltimore 5, Md.

Subcommittee on Medical Nutrition

Dr. J. S. McLESTER	(Chm.), Prof. Med., Univ. Alabama Med. Sch. 930 S. 20th St., Birmingham 5, Ala.
Prof. C. A. ELVEHJEM	Prof. Biochemistry Univ. of Wisconsin, Madison 6, Wisc.
Dr. Norman JOLLIFFE	(Secy.), Assoc. Prof. Med., N.Y. Univ. Coll. Med. 39 East 75th St., New York City
Dr. C. G. KING	Scientific Director, Nutrition Foundation Chrysler Building, New York City
Dr. David T. SMITH	Assoc. Prof. Med., Duke Univ. Med. Sch. Duke Hospital, Durham, N.C.
Dr. Frederick J. STARE	Asst. Prof. Nutrition, Harvard Medical School 25 Shattuck St., Boston 15, Mass.
Dr. V. P. SYDENSTRICKER	Prof. Med. Univ. Georgia Med. Sch., Augusta, Ga.
Dr. Russell M. WILDER	Prof. Med. & Nutr., Univ. Minn. Grad. Med. Sch. Mayo Clinic, Rochester, Minn.

Subcommittee on Tropical Diseases

Dr. Henry E. MELENEY	(Chm.), Hermann M. Biggs Prof. Prev. Med., New York Univ. Med. Sch. 477 First Avenue, New York 16, N.Y.
Dr. Mark F. BOYD	Station for Malaria Research Rockefeller Foundation, Tallahassee, Florida
Dr. Harold W. BROWN	Prof. Parasitology, Columbia University De Lamar Inst. Pub. Health 600 W. 168th St., New York 32, N.Y.
Dr. W. W. CORT	Prof. Parasitology, Johns Hopkins University 615 N. Wolfe St., Baltimore, Md.
Dr. Karl F. MEYER	The George Williams Hooper Foundation The Medical Center, San Francisco 22, Calif.
Dr. George K. STRODE	Assoc. Director, International Health Division Rockefeller Foundation New York 13, N.Y.
Dr. W. H. TALIAFERRO	Dean Division of Biological Sciences, Univ. of Chicago, Chicago 37, Ill.
Dr. H. B. van DYKE	The Squibb Institute for Medical Research New Brunswick, N.J.
Dr. Robert B. WATSON	Assoc. Prof. Prev. Med. Univ. Tenn. Sch. of Med., Memphis, Tenn.
Dr. A. Ashley WEECH	B. K. Rachford Prof. Ped., Med. Coll. of Ohio Children's Hospital, Cincinnati 29, Ohio

Subcommittee on Tuberculosis

Dr. James Burns AMBERSON, Jr.	(Chm.), Prof. Med., Col. Univ. Coll. Phys. & Surg. 415 East 26th St., New York City
Dr. Bruce H. DOUGLAS	Prof. Prev. Med. & Pub. Health, Wayne Univ. Coll. of Med. 3919 John R St., Detroit, Mich.
Dr. Herbert R. EDWARDS	Chief, Tuberculosis Div., Dept. of Health 125 Worth St., New York City
Dr. Leroy U. GARDNER	Director The Saranac Laboratory, Saranac Lake, N.Y.
Dr. Paul P. McCAIN	Asst. Prof. Med., Duke Univ. Sch. Med. Sanatorium, N. C.
Dr. J. A. MYERS	Prof. Int. Med., Prev. Med. & Pub. Health, Univ. Minn. Med. School 730 Lasalle Building, Minneapolis, Minn.
Dr. James J. WARING	Prof. Med., Univ. Colo. Sch. of Med. 4200 E. 9th Ave., Denver, Colorado

Subcommittee on Venereal Diseases

Dr. J. E. MOORE	(Chm.), Assoc. Prof. Med., Johns Hop., Univ. Sch. Medicine 804 Medical Arts Bldg., Baltimore 1, Md.
Dr. Charles W. CLARKE	American Soc. Hygiene Assoc., N.Y. 1790 Broadway, New York City
Dr. Oscar F. COX, Jr.	Secy., A. Neiserrian Soc. 1101 Beacon St., Brookline, Mass.
Dr. J. F. MAHONEY	Venereal Disease Research Laboratory Staten Island 4, N.Y.
Dr. Nels NELSON	Johns Hopkins Univ. Sch. of Public Health 4228 Kelway Road, Baltimore 18, Md.
Dr. John H. STOKES	Prof. Cut. Med. & Syph., Univ. Pa. Sch. of Med. 4228 Spruce St., Philadelphia, Pa.
Dr. Evan W. THOMAS	Prof. Med., Derm. & Syph., N.Y. Univ. Med. Coll. Rapid Treatment Center, Bellevue Hospital 26th St. & First Ave., New York City

NEUROPSYCHIATRY

Dr. Winfred OVERHOLSER	(Chm.), Prof. Psychiatry, Geo. Wash. Univ.Sch.Med. St. Elizabeths Hospital, Washington 20, D. C.
Dr. Karl M. BOWMAN	Prof. Psychiatry, Univ. Calif. Med. Sch. The Langley Porter Clinic, San Francisco 22, California
Dr. Foster KENNEDY	Prof. Clin. Med. (Neurology), Cornell Univ. Med. College 410 East 57th St., New York City
Dr. Adolf MEYER	Prof. Emer. of Psych., Johns Hop. Univ. Sch. Med. 4305 Rugby Road, Baltimore 10, Md.
Dr. Tracy J. PUTNAM	Prof. Neur. & Neurosurg., Col. Univ. Coll. Phys. & Surg. 710 W. 168th St., New York 32, N.Y.
Dr. Arthur RUGGLES	Clin. Prof. Psych. & Mental Hygiene, Yale Univ. Sch. of Med. 305 Blackstone Blvd., Providence, R.I.
Dr. Harry A. STECKEL	Prof. Psychiatry, Syracuse Univ. Coll. Med. 708 Irving Avenue, Syracuse, N.Y.
Dr. John C. WHITEHORN	(Secy.), Henry Phipps Prof. Psychiatry, Johns Hopkins Univ. Sch. Med. Johns Hopkins Hospital, Baltimore 5, Md.

Subcommittee on Neurology

Dr. Foster KENNEDY	(Chm.), Prof. Clin. Med. (Neurology), Cornell Univ. Med. College 410 East 57th St., New York City
Dr. Bernard J. ALPERS	Prof. Neurology, Jefferson Medical College 111 North 49th St., Philadelphia, Pa.
Dr. Lewis J. POLLOCK	Prof. Nerv. & Mental Diseases, Northwestern Univ. Medical School 122 S. Michigan Blvd., Chicago, Ill.
Dr. Henry A. RILEY	(Secy.), Prof. Clin. Neurology, Col. Univ. Coll. Phys. & Surg. 117 East 72nd St., New York City
Dr. David M. RIOCH	Chestnut Lodge Sanitarium, Rockville, Md.
Dr. Sidney I. SCHWAB	Prof. Clin. Neur., Wash. Univ. Sch. Med. 3720 Washington Blvd., St. Louis, Mo.
Dr. Harry C. SOLOMON	Prof. Psych., Harvard Medical School 74 Fenwood Road, Boston, Mass.

Subcommittee on Psychiatry

Dr. Arthur RUGGLES	(Chm.), Clin. Prof. Psych. & Mental Hygiene, Yale Univ. Sch. of Med. 305 Blackstone Blvd., Providence, R.I.
Dr. Frank FREMONT-SMITH	Dir., Josiah Macy, Jr. Foundation 565 Park Avenue, New York 21, N.Y.
Dr. R. Finley GAYLE	Prof. Neuropsych. Medical College of Va., Richmond 19, Va.
Dr. Roscoe W. HALL	Prof. Clin. Psych., Geo. Wash. Univ. Sch. of Med. St. Elizabeths Hospital, Washington 20, D.C
Dr. Titus HARRIS	Prof. Neuropsych., Univ. of Texas 816 Strand St., Galveston, Texas
Dr. Lawrence S. KUBIE	7 East 81st St., New York 28, N.Y.
Dr. Nolan D. C. LEWIS	Prof. Psychiatry, Col. Univ. Coll. Phys. & Surg. 722 West 168th St., New York 32, N.Y.
Dr. Edward A. STRECKER	(Secy.), Prof. Psych., Univ. Pa. Sch. of Med. 111 North 49th St., Philadelphia, Pa.

PATHOLOGY

Dr. Howard T. KARSNER	(Chm.), Prof. Path., Western Res. Univ. Sch. Med. 2085 Adelbert Road, Cleveland 6, Ohio
Dr. Paul R. CANNON	Prof. Pathology Univ. of Chicago, Chicago, Ill.
Dr. Robert A. MOORE	Edward Mallinckrodt Prof. Path. Washington Univ. Med. Sch., St. Louis, Mo.
Dr. Alwin M. PAPPENHEIMER	Prof. Path., Col. Univ. Coll. Phys. & Surg. 630 West 168th St., New York 32, N.Y.
Dr. S. Burt WOLBACH	Shattuck Prof. Path. Anat., Harvard Med. School 25 Shattuck St., Boston 15, Mass.

SANITARY ENGINEERING

Dr. Abel WOLMAN	(Chm.), Prof. Sanitary Engineering Johns Hopkins Univ., Baltimore 18, Md.
Mr. Harold E. BABBITT	Prof. Sanitary Engineering Univ. of Illinois, Urbana, Ill.
Dr. F. C. BISHOPP	Asst. Chief, Bureau of Entomology & Plant Quarantine U. S. Department of Agriculture, Washington 25,D.C.
Mr. V. M. EHLERS	Texas State Board of Health, Austin 2, Texas
Dr. Gordon M. FAIR	Gordon McKay Prof. Sanit. Sciences, Harvard Univ. 112 Pierce Hall Harvard University, Cambridge 38, Mass.
Dr. Kennery F. MAXCY	Prof. Epidemiology Johns Hopkins Univ. Sch. of Hyg. & Pub. Health Baltimore 5, Md.
Mr. H. A. WHITTAKER	Dir., Division of Sanitation Minnesota Department of Health, University Campus, Minneapolis 14, Minn.

SHOCK AND TRANSFUSIONS

Dr. Walter B. CANNON	(Chm.), Prof. Physiology (Emer.), Harvard Med. Sch. (from May 1-Nov.1, 1944) R.F.D. #1, Franklin, New Hampshire (after Nov. 1, 1944) 20 Prescott Street, Cambridge, Mass.
Dr. Alfred BLALOCK	Prof. Surg., Johns Hop. Univ. Sch. Med. Johns Hopkins Hospital, Baltimore 5, Md.
Dr. Philip BARD	Prof. Physiology Johns Hopkins Univ. Sch. Med., Baltimore 5, Md.
Dr. Donald D. VAN SLYKE	The Hospital of the Rockefeller Institute for Medical Research New York 21, N.Y.
Dr. Joseph T. WEARN	Prof. Med., Western Reserve Univ. Med. Sch. 2065 Adelbert Road, Cleveland 6, Ohio

Subcommittee on Blood Substitutes

Dr. Joseph T. WEARN	(Chm.), Prof. Med., Western Res. Univ. Med. Sch. 2065 Adelbert Road, Cleveland 6, Ohio
Dr. Edwin J. COHN	Prof. Biol. Chem.,Harvard Med. School 25 Shattuck St., Boston 15, Mass.
Dr. Elmer L. DeGOWIN	(Secy.), Res. Asst. Prof. Theory & Prac., State Univ. Iowa Coll. Med. University Hospitals, Iowa City, Iowa
Dr. Max M STRUMIA	Asst. Prof. Path., Univ. Pa. Grad. Sch. Med. Bryn Mawr, Pa.
Dr. Owen H. WANGENSTEEN	Prof. Gen. Surg., Univ. Minn. Med. Sch. 412 Delaware Street, S.W., Minneapolis, Minn.

Dr. Magnus GREGERSEN	Prof. Physiology Columbia Univ. Coll. Phys. & Surg. New York 32, N.Y.
Dr. C. N. H. LONG	Sterling Prof. Physiological Chemistry Yale Univ. Sch. Med., New Haven 11, Conn.
Dr. Joseph T. WEARN	Prof. Med., Western Reserve Univ. Med. Sch. 2065 Adelbert Road, Cleveland 6, Ohio

<u>SURGERY</u>

Dr. Evarts A. GRAHAM	(Chm.), Bixby Prof. Surg., Wash. Univ. Sch. Med. 600 S. Kingshighway, St. Louis 10, Mo.
Dr. Irvin ABELL	Clin. Prof. Surg., Univ. Louisville Med. School 321 W. Broadway, Louisville, Ky.
Dr. Donald C. BALFOUR	Prof. Surg., Univ. Minn. Grad. School Mayo Clinic, Rochester, Minn.
Dr. George E. BENNETT	Adj. Prof. Orth. Surg., Johns Hop. Univ. Sch. Med. 4 East Madison St., Baltimore, Md.
Dr. Warren H. COLE	(Secy.), Prof. Surg., Univ. Ill. Coll. of Med. 1853 W. Polk St., Chicago 12, Ill.
Dr. Frederick A. COLLER	Prof. Surg., Univ. Mich. Med. Sch. 1313 E. Ann Street, Ann Arbor, Mich.
Dr. Robert H. IVY	Prof. Maxillofacial Surg., Univ. Pa. Sch. Med. 1930 Chestnut St., Philadelphia, Pa.
Dr. Charles G. MIXTER	Clin. Prof. Surg., Harvard Med. School 319 Longwood Ave., Boston, Mass.
Dr. Howard C. NAFFZIGER	Prof. Surg., Univ. Calif. Med. School Univ. Calif. Hospital, San Francisco 22, Calif.
Dr. Alton OCHSNER	Wm. Henderson Prof. Surg., Tulane Univ. Sch. Med. 1430 Tulane Ave., New Orleans 13, La.
Dr. Allen O. WHIPPLE	Valentine Mott Prof. Surg., Col. Univ. Coll. Phys. & Surg. 180 Ft. Washington Ave., New York 32, N.Y.

<u>Subcommittee on Anesthesia</u>

Dr. Ralph M. WATERS	(Chm.), Prof. Anes., Univ. Wisc. Med. Sch. 1300 University Ave., Madison, Wisconsin
Dr. Lewis S. BOOTH	Attending Anes., Doctor's and Roosevelt Hospital 149 East 73rd St., New York City
Dr. John S. LUNDY	Prof. Anes. & Surg., Univ. Minn. Grad. Sch. Mayo Clinic, Rochester, Minn.
Dr. Emery A. ROVENSTINE	(Secy.), Prof. Anes., N.Y. Univ. Coll. Med. 477 First Ave., New York 16, N.Y.
Dr. Paul M. WOOD	Asst. Clin. Prof. Anes., N.Y. Med. College 131 Riverside Drive, New York City

Subcommittee on Infected Wounds and Burns

Dr. Allen O. WHIPPLE	(Chm.), Valentine Mott Prof. Surg., Col. Univ. Coll. Phys. & Surg. 180 Ft. Washington Ave., New York 32, N.Y.
Dr. Guy A. CALDWELL	Prof. Orth. Surg., Tulane Univ. Sch. of Med. 3503 Prytania St., New Orleans, La.
Dr. Oliver COPE	Asst. Prof. Surg., Harvard Med. School Massachusetts General Hospital, Boston, 14, Mass.
Dr. Rene J. Dubos	The Rockefeller Institute for Medical Research 66th St. & York Ave., New York 21, N.Y.
Dr. Robert ELMAN	Assoc. Prof. Clin. Surg., Wash. Univ. Sch. of Med. 600 S. Kingshighway, St. Louis 10, Mo.
Dr. Warfield M. FIROR	Assoc. Prof. Surg. Johns Hopkins Univ. Sch. Med., Baltimore 5, Md.
Dr. Edward L. Howes	Assoc. Clin.Prof.Surg., Col.Univ.Coll.Phys. & Surg. 5012 Waldo Avenue, New York 63, N.Y.
Dr. Sumner KOCH	Assoc. Prof. Surg., Northwestern Univ. Med. Sch. 54 E. Erie St., Chicago 11, Ill.
Dr. John S. LOCKWOOD	Assoc. Prof. Surg., Yale Univ. Sch. of Med. 2101 Constitution Ave., Washington 25, D. C.
Dr. Charles C. LUND	Asst. Prof. Surg., Harvard Medical School 319 Longwood Ave., Boston, 15, Mass.
Dr. Roy D. McCLURE	Henry Ford Hospital 2799 W. Grand Blvd., Detroit 2, Mich.
Dr. Frank L. MELENEY	Assoc. Prof. Clin. Surg., Col. Univ. Coll. Phys. & Surg. Presbyterian Hospital, New York City

Subcommittee on Neurosurgery

Dr. Howard C. NAFFZIGER	(Chm.), Prof. Surg., Univ. Calif. Med. School Univ. Calif. Hospital, San Francisco 22, Calif.
Dr. Claude C. COLEMAN	Prof. Neurosurg., Med. Coll. of Virginia 1200 E. Broad St., Richmond, 19, Va.
Dr. Gilbert HORRAX	605 Commonwealth Ave., Boston, Mass.
Dr. Cobb PILCHER	Assoc. Prof. Surg., Vanderbilt Univ. Med. Sch. Vanderbilt Univ. Hospital, Nashville, Tenn.
Dr. Tracy J. PUTNAM	Prof. Neuro. & Neurosurg., Col. Univ. Coll. Phys. & Surg. 710 W. 168th St., New York 32, N.Y.

Subcommittee on Ophthalmology

Dr. Harry S. GRADLE	(Chm.), Prof. Ophth. (Extra Mural), Northwestern Univ. Med. Sch. 58 East Washington St., Chicago 2, Ill.
Dr. Wm. L. BENEDICT	Prof. Ophth., Univ. Minn. Grad. School Mayo Clinic, Rochester, Minn.
Dr. Fred C. CORDES	Clin. Prof. Ophth., Univ. Calif. Med. Sch. 384 Post St., San Francisco, California
Dr. Lawrence T. POST	Prof. Clin. Ophth., Wash. Univ. Sch. of Med. 508 N. Grand Blvd., St. Louis, Mo.
Dr. Algernon B. REESE	Assoc. Clin. Prof. Ophth., Col. Univ. Coll. Phys. & Surg. 73 East 71st St., New York City
Dr. A. D. RUEDEMANN	Cleveland Clinic Euclid Ave. at 93rd St., Cleveland 6, Ohio
Dr. Alan C. WOODS	Acting Prof. Ophth., Johns Hopkins Univ. Med. Sch. Johns Hopkins Hospital, Baltimore 5, Md.

Subcommittee on Orthopedic Surgery

Dr. George E. BENNETT	(Chm.), Adj. Prof. Orth. Surg., Johns Hopkins Univ. Sch. Med. 4 East Madison St., Baltimore, Md.
Dr. LeRoy C. ABBOTT	Prof. Orth. Surg., Univ. Calif. Med. School 384 Post St., San Francisco, Calif.
Dr. Harold R. CONN	Surg. in Chief, Goodyear Tire & Rubber Co. 1144 E. Market St., Akron, Ohio
Dr. Frank D. DICKSON	Assoc. Prof. Clin. Surg., Univ. Kans Sch. of Med. 1103 Grand Ave., Kansas City, Mo.
Dr. William DARRACH	Dean Emer. & Prof. Clin. Surg., Col. Univ. Coll. Phys. & Surg. 180 Ft. Washington Ave., New York 32, N.Y.
Dr. J. Albert KEY	Prof. Clin. Orth. Surg., Wash. Univ. Sch. Med. 4952 Maryland Ave., St. Louis, Mo.
Dr. Frederick C. KIDNER	Prof. Clin. Orth. Surg., Wayne Univ. Coll. Med. 1553 Woodward Ave., Detroit, Mich.
Dr. Guy W. LEADBETTER	(Secy.), Clin. Prof. Surg., Geo. Wash. Univ. Sch.Med. 901 - 16th St., N.W., Washington 6, D. C.
Dr. Paul B. MAGNUSON	Assoc. Prof. Surg., Northwestern Univ. Med. Sch. 700 N. Michigan Blvd., Chicago,11, Ill.
Dr. Frank OBER	John Ball and Buckminster Brown Clin. Prof. Orth. Surg., Harvard Medical School 234 Marlborough St., Boston, Mass.
Dr. M. N. SMITH-PETERSEN	Clin. Prof. Orth. Surg., Harvard Medical School 264 Beacon St., Boston, Mass.
Dr. Philip D. WILSON	Clin. Prof. Orth. Surg., Col. Univ. Coll. Phys. & Surg. 321 E. 42nd St., New York City

Subcommittee on Otolaryngology

Dr. A. C. FURSTENBERG	(Chm.), Dean & Prof. Otolaryngology Univ. Mich. Med. Sch., Ann Arbor, Mich.
Dr. John MacKenzie BROWN	Clin. Prof. Surg. (Otorhinlaryn.), Univ. South. Calif. Sch. of Med. 1136 West 6th St., Los Angeles, Calif.
Dr. Stacy R. GUILD	Assoc. Prof. Otolaryng, Johns Hop. Univ. Sch. Med. Johns Hopkins Hospital, Baltimore 5, Md.
Dr. Arthur C. JONES	105 North 8th St., Boise, Idaho
Dr. Francis Ernest LE JEUNE	Prof. Otolaryng., Tulane Univ. Sch. of Med. 3503 Prytania St., New Orleans, La.
Dr. Dean McAllister LIERLE	Prof. Otolaryng., State Univ. Ia. Coll. Med. University Hospitals, Iowa City, Iowa
Dr. Fletcher Drummond WOODWARD	Prof. Dis. Ear, Nose, Throat, Univ. Va. Dept. Med. 104 E. Market St., Charlottesville, Va.

Subcommittee on Physical Therapy

Dr. John S. COULTER	(Chm.), Assoc. Prof. Phys. Ther., Northwestern Univ. Med. Sch. 122 S. Michigan Blvd., Chicago, Ill.
Dr. Frank H. EWERHARDT	Asst. Prof. Phys. Ther., Wash. Univ. Sch. of Med. 600 S. Kingshighway, St. Louis 10, Mo.
Dr. Kristian G. HANSSON	Asst. Prof. Clin. Surg. (Orth.), Cornell Univ. Medical College 33 East 61st St., New York City
Dr. Frank H. KRUSEN	(Secy.), Prof. Phys. Med., Univ. Minn. Grad. Sch. Mayo Clinic, Rochester, Minn.
Dr. Walter J. ZEITER	In charge Phys. Ther. Cleveland Clinic 2020 East 93rd St., Cleveland, Ohio

Subcommittee on Plastic and Maxillofacial Surgery

Dr. Robert H. IVY	(Chm.), Prof. Maxillofacial Surg., Univ. Pa. School of Medicine 1930 Chestnut St., Philadelphia, Pa.
Dr. John Staige DAVIS	Assoc. Prof. Surg., Johns Hopkins Sch. of Med. 701 Cathedral St., Baltimore, Md.
Joseph D. EBY, D.D.S.	121 E. 60th St., New York City
P. C. LOWERY, D.D.S.	Lowery Building, Detroit, Michigan
Dr. Ferris SMITH	1810 Wealthy Street, S.E., Grand Rapids, Michigan

Dr. Wm. Edward CHAMBERLAIN	Prof. Radiol. & Roent., Temple Univ. Med. Sch. 3401 N. Broad St., Philadelphia, Pa.
Dr. Byrl R. KIRKLIN	(Secy.), Assoc. Prof. Radiol., Univ.Minn. Grad.Sch. Mayo Clinic, Rochester, Minn.
Dr. Ursus Victor PORTMANN	2020 E. 93rd St., Cleveland, Ohio
Dr. Eugene P. PENDERGRASS	Prof. Radiol., Univ. Pa. Med. School 3400 Spruce St., Philadelphia, Pa.

Subcommittee on Thoracic Surgery

Dr. Evarts A. GRAHAM	(Chm.), Bixby Prof. Surg., Wash. Univ. Sch. Med. 600 S. Kingshighway, St. Louis 10, Mo.
Dr. John ALEXANDER	Prof. Surg., Univ. Mich. Med. Sch. 1313 E. Ann St., Ann Arbor, Mich.
Dr. Isaac A. BIGGER	Prof. Surg., Med. Coll. of Virginia 1200 E. Broad St., Richmond, Virginia
Dr. Leo ELOESSER	Clin. Prof. Surg., Stanford Univ. Sch. of Med. 490 Post Street, San Francisco, Calif.

Subcommittee on Urology

Dr. Herman L. KRETSCHMER	(Chm.), Prof. Urol., Rush College of Medicine 122 S. Michigan Blvd. Chicago, Illinois
Dr. William F. BRAASCH	Prof. Urol., Univ. Minn. Grad. Sch. Mayo Clinic, Rochester, Minn.
Dr. H. G. HAMER	Clin. Prof. G.U. Surg., Indiana Univ. Sch. Med. 1711 N. Capitol Ave., Indianapolis, Indiana
Dr. Frank HINMAN	Clin. Prof. Urol., Univ. Calif. Med. Sch. 384 Post St., San Francisco, Calif.
Dr. Chas. Brenton HUGGINS	Prof. Surg. (Urol.), Univ. Chicago Sch. Med. 950 East 59th St., Chicago, Ill.
Dr. Albert J. SCHOLL	Assoc. Clin. Prof. Surg. (Urol.), Univ. South. Calif. Med. School 1930 Wilshire Blvd., Los Angeles, Calif.

Subcommittee on Vascular Injuries

Dr. John HOMANS	(Chm.), Clin. Prof. Surg. (Emer.), Harvard Med. Sch. 311 Beacon St., Boston, Mass.
Dr. Arthur W. ALLEN	Lect. on Surg., Harvard Medical School 264 Beacon St., Boston, Mass.
Dr. Geza de TAKATS	Assoc. Prof. Surg., Univ. Ill. Coll. of Med. 122 S. Michigan Blvd., Chicago, Ill.
Dr. J. Ross VEAL	Adj. Clin. Prof. Surg., Geo. Wash. Univ. Med. Sch. Gallinger Municipal Hospital, Washington 3, D.C.

TREATMENT OF GAS CASUALTIES

Dr. Milton C. WINTERNITZ	(Chm.), Anthony N. Brady Prof. Path., Yale Univ. School of Medicine 310 Cedar St., New Haven 11, Conn.
Dr. David P. BARR	Prof. Med., Cornell Univ. Med. College York Ave. and 68th St., New York City
Dr. Wm. Mansfield CLARK	Prof. Phys. Chem., Johns Hopkins Univ. Sch. Med. 2101 Constitution Ave., Washington 25, D. C.

BOARD FOR THE COORDINATION OF MALARIAL STUDIES

Dr. Robert F. LOEB	(Chm.), Lambert Prof. Med., Columbia Univ. Coll. Phys. & Surg. 622 W. 168th St., New York 32, N.Y.
Dr. George A. CARDEN, Jr.	(Secy.), 2101 Constitution Avenue, Washington 25, D. C.
Dr. Wm. Mansfield CLARK	Prof. Physiological Chem., Johns Hop. Univ. Sch. Med. 2101 Constitution Ave., Washington 25, D.C.
Dr. G. Robert COATNEY	Senior Protozoologist, U. S. Public Health Service National Institute of Health, Bethesda 14, Md.
Comdr. L. T. COGGESHALL (MC) USNR	Senior Medical Officer Marine Barracks, Klamath Falls, Oregon
Lt. Col. Francis R. DIEUAIDE, M.C., AUS	Office of the Surgeon General 1818 H St., N.W., Washington 25, D. C.
Dr. A. R. DOCHEZ	John E. Borne Prof. Med. & Surg. Res., Columbia Univ. Coll. Phys. & Surg. 700 West 168th St., New York, 32, N.Y.
Capt. E. G. HAKANSSON (MC), USN	Naval Medical Research Institute Bethesda 14, Md.
Dr. E. K. MARSHALL, Jr.	Prof. Pharm. & Exp. Ther., Johns Hopkins Univ. School of Medicine Baltimore 5, Md.
Dr. C. S. MARVEL	Prof. Organic Chemistry, Univ. of Ill. Noyes Laboratory, Urbana, Illinois
Major O. R. McCOY, M.C., AUS	Office of the Surgeon General 1818 H St., N.W., Washington 25, D. C.
Lt. Comdr. Frank T. NORRIS (MC), USN	Bureau of Medicine & Surgery Navy Department, Washington 25, D. C.
Dr. W. H. SEBRELL	Senior Surgeon, U. S. Public Health Service National Institute of Health, Bethesda 14, Md.
Dr. James A. SHANNON	Prof. Pharm., N.Y. Univ. Coll. Med. Goldwater Memorial Hospital, Welfare Island 17, New York City

Panel on Clinical Testing of Antimalarials

Dr. James A. SHANNON	(Chm.), Prof. Pharm., N.Y. Univ. Coll. Med. Goldwater Memorial Hospital, Welfare Island 17, New York City
Dr. Alf S. ALVING	Assoc. Prof. Med., Univ. Chicago Frank Billings Medical Clinic, Chicago 37, Ill.
Dr. Francis G. BLAKE	Sterling Prof. Med. Yale Univ. Sch. of Med., New Haven 11, Conn.
Dr. Allan M. BUTLER	Asst. Prof. Ped., Harvard Medical School Mass. General Hospital, Boston 14, Mass.
Dr. W. Clark COOPER	P. A. Surgeon U. S. Public Health Service, Bethesda 14, Md.
Dr. Robert F. LOEB (ex officio)	Lambert Prof. Med., Col. Univ. Coll. Phys. & Surg. 622 West 168th St., New York 32, N.Y.
Dr. Donald D. VAN SLYKE	Rockefeller Institute for Medical Research 66th St. and York Ave., New York 21, N.Y.
Dr. Robert B. WATSON	Assoc. Prof. Prev. Med. Univ. Tenn. Sch. of Med., Memphis, Tenn.

Panel on Pharmacology of Antimalarials

Dr. E. K. MARSHALL, Jr.	(Chm.), Prof. Pharm. & Exp. Ther. Johns Hopkins Univ. Sch. Med., Baltimore 5, Md.
Dr. Thomas C. BUTLER	(Secy.), Johns Hopkins Univ. Sch. Med. Baltimore 5, Md.
Dr. G. Robert COATNEY	Senior Protozoologist, U. S. Public Health Service National Institute of Health, Bethesda 14, Md.
Dr. E. M. K. GEILING	Prof. Pharmacology University of Chicago, Chicago 37, Ill.
Dr. Robert F. LOEB (ex officio)	Lambert Prof. Med., Col. Univ. Coll. Phys. & Surg. 622 West 168th St., New York 32, N.Y.
Dr. Richard J. PORTER	Instr. Epidemiology Univ. Mich. Sch. of Med., Ann Arbor, Mich.
Dr. Leon H. SCHMIDT	Dir. Inst. for Med. Research The Christ Hospital, Cincinnati 19, Ohio
Dr. W. H. TALIAFERRO	Dean, Division of Biological Sciences University of Chicago, Chicago 37, Ill.

Panel on Biochemistry of Antimalarials
(Division of Chemistry)

Dr. Wm. Mansfield CLARK	(Chm.), Prof. Phys. Chem., Johns Hop. Univ. Sch.Med. 2101 Constitution Ave., Washington 25, D.C.
Dr. Eric G. BALL	Assoc. Prof. Biochemistry Harvard Medical School, Boston 15, Mass.
Dr. Vincent du VIGNEAUD	Prof. Biochemistry, Cornell Univ. Med. Coll. 1300 York Ave., New York City
Dr. Robert F. LOEB (ex officio)	Lambert Prof. Med., Col. Univ. Coll. Phys. & Surg. 622 West 168th St., New York 32, N.Y.
Dr. W. H. TALIAFERRO	Dean, Division of Biological Sciences University of Chicago, Chicago 37, Ill.
Dr. Kenneth C. BLANCHARD	Survey of Antimalarial Drugs 710 N. Washington St., Baltimore 5, Md.

Panel on Synthesis of Antimalarials
(Division of Chemistry)

Dr. C. S. MARVEL	(Chm.), Prof. Organic Chem., Univ. of Illinois Noyes Laboratory, Urbana, Ill.
Dr. Kenneth C. BLANCHARD	Survey of Antimalarial Drugs 710 N. Washington St., Baltimore 5, Md.
Dr. Arthur COPE	Assoc. Prof. Organic Chem., Columbia University Chandler Laboratory, New York 27, N.Y.
Dr. N. L. DRAKE	Prof. Organic Chemistry Univ. of Maryland, College Park, Md.
Dr. Robert ELDERFIELD	(Secy.), Prof. Chem., Columbia University Chandler Laboratory, New York 27, N.Y.
Dr. Joseph B. KOEPFLI	Res. Assoc. in Chemistry Calif. Inst. of Technology, Pasadena 4, Calif.
Dr. Robert F. LOEB (ex officio)	Lambert Prof. Med., Col. Univ. Coll. Phys. & Surg. 622 West 168th St., New York 32, N.Y.
Dr. Ralph L. SHRINER	Chairman, Dept. of Chemistry Indiana Univ., Bloomington, Ind.
Dr. Lyndon SMALL	Head Chemist, Division of Chemotherapy, U.S. Public Health Service National Institute of Health, Bethesda 14, Md.
Dr. Frederick Y. WISELOGLE	Survey of Antimalarial Drugs 710 N. Washington St., Baltimore 5, Md.

... CORE	Assoc. Prof. Organic Chem., Columbia University Chandler Laboratory, New York 27, N.Y.
... DRAKE	Prof. Organic Chemistry Univ. of Maryland, College Park, Md.
... ELDERFIELD	(Secy.), Prof. Chem., Columbia University Chandler Laboratory, New York 27, N.Y.
... B. KOEPFLI	Res. Assoc. in Chemistry Calif. Inst. of Technology, Pasadena 4, Calif.
... F. LOEB (...field)	Lambert Prof. Med., Col. Univ. Coll. Phys. & Surg. 622 West 168th St., New York 32, N.Y.
... ENDINE	Chairman, Dept. of Chemistry Indiana Univ., Bloomington, Ind.
... SMALL	Head Chemist, Division of Chemotherapy, U.S. Public Health Service National Institute of Health, Bethesda 14, Md.
... F. WISELOGLE	Survey of Antimalarial Drugs 710 N. Washington St., Baltimore 5, Md.

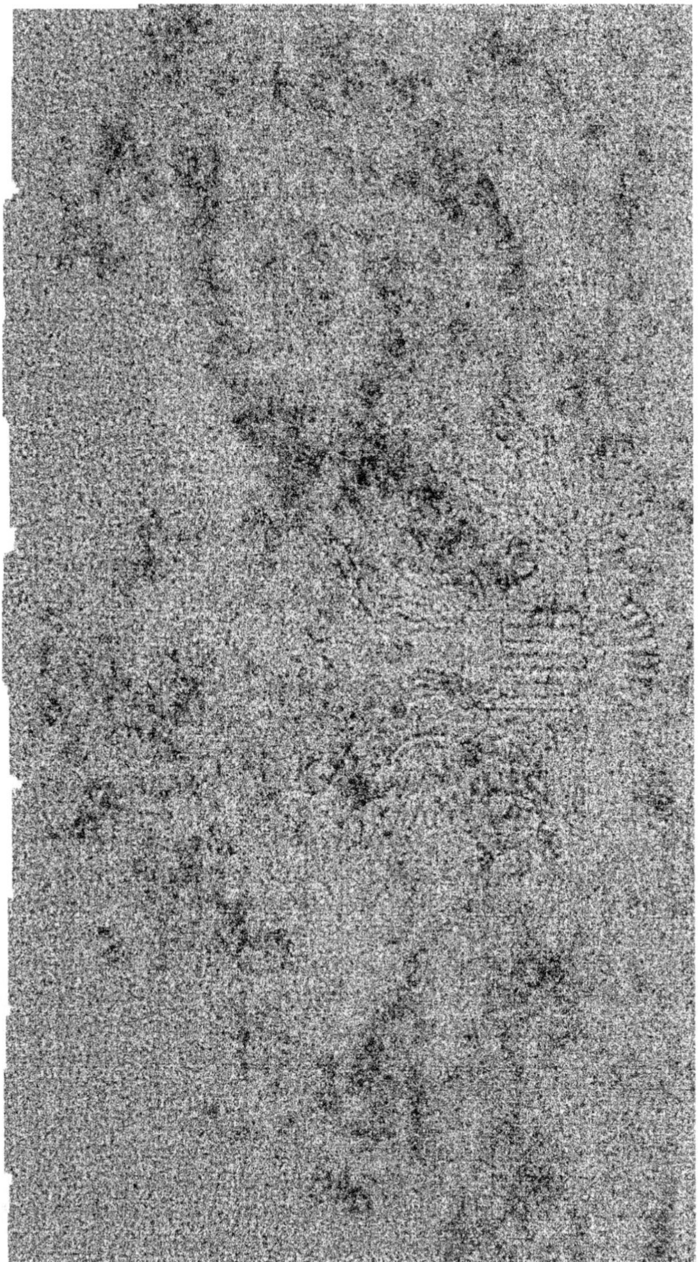

CPSIA information can be obtained
at www.ICGtesting.com
Printed in the USA
BVHW041435220219
540923BV00007B/476/P

9 781397 312969